WHAT DOES OUR LADY SOUND LIKE?

A FIRST PERSON ACCOUNT

JUDE D'SOUZA

This book is dedicated to my heavenly virgin mother for prodding and inspiring me to bring out many such interesting, inspiring, thought-provoking content-laden works to the faithful. It would never have been possible without her constant guidance and eye on my career. She is over-zealous to honour me in my spiritual journey to the ultimate goal of reaching heavenly bliss- a goal that seems elusive to many but a very part of me through his grace.

Contents

Foreword

I have known Jude D'Souza for quite a decade, since he first stepped into our Bangalore outreach at SRM City Centre, Hennur. His first glimpse of our gospel activity was the regular Sunday fellowship.

He seemed to be a person keeping a long desire in his eyes to avail himself of God's grace. He was well-disciplined listener of the Word of God with a philosophical mind. Many times, he expressed his keen interest in looking into the principles of the Kingdom of God.

The relationship of the author with the Lord Jesus Christ is very deep and scripturally anchored. He has a sense of belonging to the Lord through his Emmanuel experience with Jesus. He is always keeping a motherly friendship and affection with Mother Mary, always sensitive to the intuitions he receives in his heart.

When he first came up with the prospect of me writing a foreword for this memoir-themed book of his regarding Our Lady, I was quite apprehensive about the purpose and wisdom in the exercise. After being emboldened by his stance on the added professional bearing given to this book, if I obliged, I assented.

This book has 14 chapters. All of these are chosen to be very relevant to the prevalent times in our world.

As Jude is known to be very close to Our Lady in his

daily dealings, he has summarized the same relationship in these chapters with a fairly interspersed number of anecdotes from his life and occurrences around.

The attributes and nature of her pleasant voice are much discussed in this book. This book is an answer to the very common and simple question, 'What does Mother Mary sound like?' in a very beautiful and interesting way. All fourteen chapters are presented so that anyone can find the qualities of the counsel of Mother which the author heard in his conversations with her, and through how she was portrayed to him.

This book is etched with Jude's first open and candid testimony regarding his spiritual journey with the Lord. There is a very beautiful play of words about how he finds himself standing on the same pedestal as many intellectual Saints of the Catholic Church and all the hardships faced by him at par with these great people of God.

His works along with this book are published to inspire a generation of people—young and old alike—to be closer to God and seek only him without paying heed to the materialistic nature of the modern world.

As such a book that delves greatly into the characteristics and nature of the voice of Our Lady is a rarity, I encourage him to further come up with many other beautiful and prized works for the glory of God in the greater sense.

I am sure that the Holy Spirit will use Jude to explore

more mystical revelations from the Scripture and the Holy traditions of the Catholic Church. All his labour and fruits will be a blessing for the students and youth, if not for all.

May the gracious Lord empower him to enlarge the territory of his work for the people of God.

Bro Savy Joseph
Director & International Mission Head
Spiritual Revival Ministry

Jude D'Souza with his award won at KLC 2024

Introduction

This is my second book in the genre of catholic spirituality. The first one *Spiritual Truths Revealed- Unlock the Mysteries* offered readers a deep insight into the lives of Saints. The second one is about applied psychology and useful in reading minds of people through body language. The same book *The Body Language Trail* has won me an award <u>Non-Fiction Suenos Book of the Year 2023.</u>

While nothing much was shared by me in the first book about how the lives of these great people of God with a special anointing could be intricately connected to my life and how I gained such deep insight into the same, this book goes a bit deeper rather than just reference books or bible verses.

Though a lay person with the antecedents of a preacher, I'm still deeply connected to God and hear his voice, literally, all the time. Most of the time it is Mother Mary with her constant prodding, guidance, help and more. But her voice is interspersed with that of the Trinity too. Along with the voice, I get visions so as to minister to people and guidance for myself or family.

My journey

To give a brief background of how I am connected to God on a deeper level, here follows an account of the same.

I prayed to God, since the fourth grade, constantly everywhere I went. This could be: the Church; prayer meetings; retreats; rosary in family or community. As those were the days of the beginning of a new millennium and doomsday prophecies, along with other uncertainties, my prayer to God was to do anything that he wants with my life and somehow take me to heaven, keeping my soul unstained and pure. This was my constant prayer for a few years.

He answered this prayer through salvific suffering. I noticed the signs soon after and I bear the suffering even now—though in a milder manner— after twenty years of its onset. This trait is similar to what the great Saints like St Alphonsa or many others experienced. Though it was largely present in every one of these specially anointed people of God, somehow the fact has—with much intrigue—escaped being recorded in history or books.

As the phrase goes, 'history repeats itself', so is the case in these illustrious people's lives. All of the Saints had stark similarities between each other: they were babied in their community like St Therese of Lisieux or St Thomas Aquinas because of their chaste nature and innocence to many evils around; felt that their lives are similar like St Edith Stein did; knew every detail of their death beforehand like, again, St Edith Stein; had a long psychological illness like St Alphonsa; people called them 'dumb ox' for quite an amount of time like St Thomas Aquinas; were very serious about their prayer and not sad, but joyous about their death like St Therese of Lisieux; were considered Saints while they were still alive like St Anthony of Padua; did not approve of publicity regarding their spiritual phenomena or gifts like St Padre

Pio with his stigmata; experienced a very tiresome feeling when they went against God's will and Mother's words like Sts Jacinta and Francesco and many more. The list can go on and on.

It is the same in my life too. I find my life similar to that of the intellectual Saints.

Coming back to the suffering part of my life, even St Therese of Lisieux too had a nervous disorder from her childhood, though not meticulously recorded. These bondages are to release souls from purgatory. In my case, as Mother said, 200 souls were released. This is the central theme in many Saints' lives and their honour is very great because they bore such sicknesses.

The suffering was a mild one but nonetheless it can be termed a malady. The grace was such that, while bearing it, there is a feeling which is persistent. It suggests that God sent the sickness in my life and only he can take it away. Also, after bearing a bout of the sickness, I felt ready to bear even more of it. I was ready for it even though it was quite unbearable. Such a grace existed in the life of great Saints as I discovered later on.

Also, as the suffering is allowed by God, there cannot be anything untoward all through the period it is borne. No one contemplates of taking down their own or their family's life through suicide. Everyone and everything are under the protection of God's mantle.

The bondages affected my academic life too. I was an above average student till my tenth grade. Slowly, in the forthcoming grades, there was a decline in my scores. It gradually worsened and I had to shelve the plans of studying further academic courses for the better as suggested by a well-known preacher that we met.

It happened thus: We reached the retreat centre- me, my dad and sister. I cried thinking of the situation I'm in—during the leisurely time of the retreat—at the place we were assigned to lodge. While having tears in my eyes, I prayed to God for a remedy.

As I was walking through the retreat hall, a bible verse on the wall flashed before me,

"I have heard your prayer,
I have seen your tears:"
Isaiah 38:5

Later, the next day, the suggestion to take a reprieve from studies was revealed as from God by the preacher. Also, she revealed to my dad that he's got a very good son.

By this time, God used to talk to me about his plans for my life through verses on the calendar at home and such.

"Do not fear, for I am with you,
Do not be dismayed, for I am your God.
I will strengthen you and help you,
I will uphold you with my righteous right hand."
Isaiah 41:10

Because I was prayerless, he couldn't do more. But he remained true to this promise and I can notice the same being fulfilled at this point of my life. It was his mind spoken to me thus.

Meanwhile, a known person began to start a tirade regarding my failures in the academic sense. He launched a smearing campaign because of some of my past distasteful happenings with his son. There was no event or programme where he did not speak about my debacle in the academic field or the cooked-up reasons for my plummeting scores. His most trusted colleague too joined the bandwagon of mudslinging.

Later I found out that the person and his colleague both succumbed to throat cancer. As I have an honour, there are some things that one is forbidden to do.

"Do not touch my anointed ones; do my prophets no harm."
Psalm 105:15 NRSVCE

Meanwhile, our family moved to a city that we presently live in on account of my dad's transfer. The bondages continued and though it was nasty at times, nothing crumbled down; everything had a sort of semblance.

I collected many promise verses from the bible that were sent to me—in the course of time—through my correspondence with a well-known preacher; they comforted me a lot during this phase and I could vaguely sense the course of God's future plans for my life. Also, during a night vigil, one preacher got a very powerful message from Jesus that someone was blabbering against the Lord.

It was me. I was doing it two days before this night vigil at home contemplating at my seemingly hopeless situation. The preacher revealed that Jesus himself spoke to him to tell a person i.e., me, that he needs some time. Though I did not testify during the night vigil that the person was me by standing up among the whole congregation while the preacher asked for it, I met the preacher later, discreetly, while he was leaving the venue to talk about it. This is because I has thought at the time that it could be anyone in the whole gathering and also, I was very unsure about myself then.

The moment I met him personally, the preacher said that it was a very powerful message from Jesus and chided me for not testifying about the same during the night vigil. He asked me to tell about this loudly among the many people who were leaving from the venue then and there. I did and people started laughing about my introversion.

The fact remains that I was prayerless all this while. But God still was working in my life waiting for the right opportunity to get me to pray for the situation that I was in. This is because though I suffered for him, he could have helped more if I prayed.

God is very patient and he waited for many years.

The opportunity came in the form of a demonic possession that I encountered on a reputed social media platform while I was debating with a very elusive person. I mocked him being misled by masquerading voices and it turned out to be a gargantuan mess.

Meanwhile, I was answering questions on the same platform for a group or community. That community was 70,000 members strong.

I kept answering all the questions I could and was known there to be endowed with God's wisdom. Also, by this time, I had gained intellectual abilities as God had promised me that he would restore twice as much [Zechariah 9:12].

The admin of that group posted that she wanted to be pure like a Saint whose picture she posted on her wall. Being nudged by Mother, I comforted her on the same thread that God will help her. When she didn't reply, I commented the second time.

Just as I said this, the admin got very angry and began to accuse me of not conforming to the Vatican II theology with her limited knowledge. All that I did was to remind her of the graces God was able to help her with.

I left the group after knowing this would snowball into something disastrous that I cannot cope up with. By evening, Jesus came to me and was enquiring about my day. I was very depressed and shared this incident. He said that he will check and returned to say that such a thread mocking me existed in the group after I left.

The mockery on the thread of the social medium was very grave and evil. Those admins compared my chaste nature to the copulatory inertness of old men and also posted hate comments with expletives. I came to know about this later.

Meanwhile, Jesus was wrathful and indignant. He comforted me and left.

Next day, I could see the admins of that group posting on their wall about whether some exotic fruits can help cure cancer. I asked Mother and she revealed that she has punished them with a very rare cancer. She had created a profile using her name and had judged this case with the said terminal illness. This was necessary—according to Jesus—because what they had done was evil and had to be punished; he also forbade me to talk anything about it on other groups and not to engage with these people. Though these admins have their own coping mechanism now, the damage is already being done.

Mother blessed many people there too, during this event and everyone one of the users of this social medium were very respectful towards me during conversations in other groups.

She also gave me a gist of the conversation of her with the punished people in the group after I asked for the same. It transpires that she sternly asked them to respect their Saints and be kind to me i.e., her son. I got to know through her talks about it and even now, I hear conversations about me that people have after I have left the place. This I do, even though the talks were between people miles away.

As in parallel universe, about my demonic possession, my bondages worsened greatly because of this encounter. I was tortured day and night, but still the grace of God existed as I'm very special to him.

*"Because you are precious in my sight, and honored, and I love you,
I give people in return for you, nations in exchange for your life."*
Isaiah 43:4 NRSVCE

During this torture, while I was lying on my bed in the room, the demon said in my ears that I should look in the mirror and he would reveal to me who he is. Just then, Jesus asked me to not look into the mirror but close my eyes. He is very fearsome and was not perturbed by what the demon could do to me.

I obeyed and closed my eyes. The demon manifested but I did not watch it.

Later, after some days, I cried and prayed. Mother used to wake me up every one and a half hour into sleep all through the night. After praying five rosaries, she sent me to sleep again saying that she will wake me up again. She did this a number of times.

The next day, I was asked by her to got to a relative's place to ask forgiveness because I had hurt her deeply. I set out in the evening. Mother was talking to me all the time that the Father is deeply hurt and I am a heavenly child.

When I reached this person's place, she stopped talking constantly. The people concerned forgave me and I returned home. This put some misunderstanding in our extended family to rest.

After a few days, I met my guardian angel who rescued me from the machinations of the Devil and the ignominious future he had prepared for me where everything was at stake. He looked just like me but a lot slimmer and with pointed features along with my brown skin tone. Mother revealed that he is my elder brother who could not be born into this world. My mother attested to it later.

He introduced to me that he was working nearby as a medical professional. Later, he took me aside to talk and asked a few questions. These questions were about my health and fitness. The moment I replied to his question about me having any addictions that I don't have any, he cried. And like any elder brother would have done, he asked me to be that way and it is good.

After some time, he left the place assuring me that he would be nearby if something untoward happens. Sure enough, I had a heavenly experience while returning from this place and Mother entered me. The experience made me have a pleasing sensation in my mind and lasted for two long hours; she talked a lot about my future as I used to be always concerned about it. But the sad part is that I forgot everything later.

Later, when I reached home, she asked me to go to mass daily. Mother said that she wants round-the-clock prayers. I was praying rosaries continuously for 15 days. She used to guide me with St Michael the Archangel about the intentions to pray right before the attack. The intentions would be a set of bondages that I had to name like prayerlessness, laziness, blasphemy, spiritual pride and such before every decade.

At the end of these 15 days, I saw a beastly figure cornered and shuddering, along with a pleasing sensation in my head. My misery ended and I was delivered.

That started the onset of me having a very rigorous personal prayer session daily. I prayed for the intention of making me more and more prayerful. I got an answer to that prayer and nowadays, I pray for almost 4–4.5 hours daily without fail.

At present, I have received a message on live television prayer meeting that I am being anointed since a few months. I have the gift of tongues and am seeing visions to minister to others; my family and myself. It has been a beautiful experience.

What qualifies me to write the book?

As guided by God, I met a renowned deliverance minister. He said that he has to discern my calling and will help me to be true to it as I need guidance for the same.

He prayed over me and revealed many things: I have a lot of inner wounds; have faced many rejections; have a genuine calling to be a preacher; God is calling me to healing ministry and that the Lord will help me.

Also, as revealed by Mother, I will be preaching in a

few weeks after being fully anointed and being clothed in power.

"And see, I am sending upon you what my Father
promised; so stay here in the city
Until you have been clothed with power from on high."
Luke 24:49 NRSVCE

I am very close to God as mentioned before and hear the voice of Mother and God constantly- literally, all the time. I feel his and her warm touch on my back gently caressing me—in the manner of kids—when I am tense or worried or upset and finding it difficult to cope with situations coming onto me. There is also a warm feeling of a kiss landing on my neck every now and then.

This was not true to all the Saints; they did not hear their voices constantly. There was a gap of days together too between the talks these great people of God had with Mother and God. This could be noticed in their diaries they have recorded- be it St Faustina Kowalska or others.

She also zealously guards my honour and says that I'm very special to her. It is the honour of a Saint and being God's son. As is being obvious, Saints are a matter of pride and blessing to their community and people around. He has inspired me from the Bible about this many times.

"I will make you the everlasting pride and joy of all
generations."
Isaiah 60:15 NIV

God has bestowed a number of graces on me daily and

sustained me during all the trying situations. I have no complaints of being under the loving gaze of such a good father.

> *"The Lord will guide you continually, and satisfy your needs in parched places,*
> *And make your bones strong; and you shall be like a watered garden,*
> *Like a spring of water, whose waters never fail."*
> *Isaiah 58:11 NRSVCE*

Why this book?

As I shared with many people around—in the church, fellowship or anywhere—regarding my calling, because everybody needs to have a testimony regarding the glorious things the Lord has done in their lives, many intriguing questions came forth from the listeners.

Before, I would not open up about any of these. I thought that it would be pride to talk about myself in this manner of being special and highly favoured by God. This false notion was laid to rest by one of the preachers who delivered a talk about the same. As understood, testimonies are to glorify God. I did the same.

One of the most common questions was what does Mother sound like. This book was inspired by the same question from a fellow church-goer I met. Also, Mother had said while talking to me some days before writing this book that I will write a book. I right away knew that it was God's will and sure enough, she would help me to do it because the same conversation with her before has ended up with me writing the previous award-winning book.

Gradually, I thought about how to present this book in a given structure and ideated a lot. Then, this book was born.

What to Find in This Book?

This book has quite a simple structure: Each chapter is presented with: the qualities of the voice of Mother I heard in conversations with her; what responses she does not give; the responses she has given and how it reveals about what she is indeed like. There is a basic introduction; then the typical statements and sentences that Mother has used or cannot do so in her conversations with me; an explanation regarding the various contexts and incidents along with anecdotes that come to mind when presented with these; and at the outset, a conclusion.

Let's begin.

CHAPTER ONE

No Air of Authority

As we see in our everyday worldly dealings with the people who are in a position of authority, they have a firm-handed approach in dealing with things. At times it may even sound that they dictate terms for us to live by. As is the common approach, we think that if they do not behave like this, then they cannot control people or exercise their authority in any aspect of duty or work.

Let this be in any context: Guardians, parents dealing with their wards or even people in teaching positions. Mother never says the below words to me:

Typical statements

1. You are to obey it; Children obey their mother
2. I forbid this; I won't allow this
3. I have authority over you

Explanations

1. Obedience

Mother never uses this phrase with me and hasn't ever till date. I feel her warmth of caring, gentle, motherly love when she expects that I obey her with the things she speaks. She knows that I'm a very loving child and am very special or rare.

She fully trusts me as parents do in a mother-son relationship. Suffice to say, a son needs to win the trust of his mother so that the relationship goes on smoothly and is nurtured to bring the loving fruits of it.

As I'm very pleasing to her. She never comes up with these phrases.

"The Lord, your God, is in your midst, a warrior who gives victory;
He will rejoice over you with gladness, he will renew you with his love;
He will exult over you with loud singing."
Zephaniah 3:17 NRSVCE

2. Forbiddance

It is a common term earthly parents use in their everyday routine with their son or daughter. If the child asks for something not fruitful, they tersely forbid the same.

I was passing by a provision store near my house quite a decade back. As we, being a family, used to live in a rented house near a renowned school and my mother used to work there, this was the usual routine of mine to come across parents and children near the institution.

A kindergarten child found a very colourful and pleasing candy at the store I just mentioned. It was nagging the parent to buy the same for her. The parent saw that the quite expensive confectionery was not fruitful for the little one and used the above term that he forbids the same.

Mother has never used the term with me and I'm quite overwhelmed by her love towards me. It is quite a reminder from her about how special I am.

3. Authority over you

Mother, also, never uses this phrase in my talks with her ever. Sometimes, I mention it to her that she has a very great office of authority. But she gently discourages me from the thought.

Many a time, I used to imagine about how she could assert her authority on the countless number of angels she has a hold over. She says that she rules over them with love and they have a choice in siding with her or anybody else- a free will.

> *"You know that the rulers of the Gentiles lord it over them,*
> *And their great ones are tyrants over them."*
> *Matthew 20:25 NRSVCE*

It is truly not so with the authorities in heaven. Mother is loving.

Conclusion

It is very hard to imagine that Mother being so gentle,

caring, loving, warm in her approach towards me or anyone can have an air of authority in her talks. She need not assert to get things done too. But only exhort or suggest to any one of the celestial angelic beings around her throne. These baby-resembling beings do it with great love for her. Great is her love towards them or her children.

Lacks Assertion

People at workplaces or the rich and affluent prove themselves to be hard taskmasters. They maintain a level of authority in words with their subordinates. Also, even in a homely setting, siblings or parents can get quite demanding with their younger ones to get things done.

This can be observed in various contexts wherein older siblings make their younger ones massage their scalp by promising candies or a trip to the bazaar. Even in the context involving parents, they make certain assertions to prove their dominance.

Mother has never done this for me or can do- be in any of the contexts below:

Typical statements

1. What was that prayer? Go and find it out.
2. Move from this place for me; hold this for me.
3. Bring this for me from this place.

Explanations

1. Whereabouts of prayer

As I said, Mother never asserts things. As some people who hold a sway over others like one's seniors in college, she never has done that to me.

Whenever I asked her in counter-question things like, 'Where can I find the prayer you just mentioned?' or 'When will I publish this book?', her typical responses are very different from earthly people. She just says that I will find out about it as I'm predestined and she leads me into things prepared beforehand through prayer.

Once, I was thinking about publishing my first book and did not know anything about how to go about it. I just started off with the hard copy of my manuscript to a publisher at a bookstore.

As I reached the place, I asked her on how to go about it. She just replied that he will help you. You could see that she didn't say, go tomorrow or at any day and 'find out'. She's thus.

2. Request work

I reckon that she also wouldn't request work to get done from me. Imagine, people at home always ask you to: pass on the tv remote control next to the place you're sitting on a sofa; to switch on the geyser for me; to switch on the fan for them from the nearby place you are sitting or anything else.

She is not like that. Even though if she does it the behaviour should be very rare or with a caring touch.

Conclusion

Mother doesn't bug me to get things done for her. As she knows everything and the future that is going to take place, she doesn't sound assertive or having a strong stance in her tone. She is gentle, forbearing and accommodative. Very soothing too.

CHAPTER THREE

No Condescension

As we see everywhere around in our daily dealings with people, there is some or the other hurtful comments from them. One of the many attitudes that people who are well-off exhibit is condescension towards their less-endowed counterparts. This could be anything from a professional perspective or in the common terms.

People like lawyers have such attitude towards the opposite party clients in their questions; some strict teachers or professors have towards their pupils; strict parents have towards their children or in the prevalent sense, God is presumed to have towards mortals.

Such condescending attitude was never showed by Mother to me, however different I was from her or not going along in my practical life with her ideals. Though she is very holy, she presumes me to be too.

Typical statements

1. You did not pray today
2. Be a good child

Explanations

1. Prayerlessness

There have been many instances where I was found to be lacking of a very good bearing for prayer. Though I was such for many years, gradually I began to show interest in intense prayers for hours together. And it has not waned down until now. I persevere strongly.

During this prayerless period, Mother was very patient with me. There was no anger as an emotion, mostly. She asked through many prayerful people—as I can remember—for me to pray and only then she could help.

One of the instances was wherein a telephonic conversation with a prayer warrior for her to pray for my troubles ended up with her reprimanding me. She asked God—in her short prayer—to remove the idleness from my life.

Nonetheless, I don't hold any grudge against this woman of God as I too would have done the same. But now, as I think, it was a kind of bondage I was entangled into.

This is what was revealed by another woman of God later in my life that Satan has done something to prevent me from praying. Later, after sensing this acute prayerlessness, she said that nothing can happen in my life if I neglected prayer the way I was doing. She meant that God can't help otherwise.

I happened to notice that she spoke with concern as to a

child- which I am.

And after this acute prayerless phase in my life that was nagging, now too, if I missed any one of my routine prayers, Mother would not scold or warn me. But she exhorts in a gentle way that she was waiting for me to pray; she says, 'Pray, son'. I oblige and start praying.

There has never been such a condescending moment from her in doing this.

2. Be a good child

Mother has always been very proud of me and has never made such a statement. She has often showed me that I am a very rare, special and good child. Also, she has revealed that there has never been such a good child in the whole world as me.

So, to make such a statement as above is atypical of her. But, rather, she has said that I'm a good child as many parents do to their children.

Conclusion

Mother can never be condescending and does not show me that she's the boss. I have never found anyone so gentle, mild, caring, loving, unassuming, forthcoming, accommodating as her. She is the ideal and perfect woman that we all can imagine as a Mother. And to put it in simpler words, she is heavenly.

CHAPTER FOUR

No Attitude

We can see numerous incidents in our daily life wherein people who are well to do, give abrasive talk or nasty, demeaning or sneering looks. This may be because of these people's belonging to the top rung of the social ladder. And even though some people are prayerful, such attitude does not escape from our observation while being with them. Though, it may be milder than the prayerless ones.

There are no instances I can remember in my life where I found Mother to show such behaviour even in a very mild manner.

Typical statements

1. Help this elderly lady
2. I'm your mother; get this thing done for me
3. Give alms to that beggar

Explanations

1. Helping the maimed

Recently, I was attending a prayer meeting and had

enough leisurely time to look around the centre admiring the landscape. It was because I had reached the place well before time and was finding it hard to stay inside and sit comfortably doing nothing.

A lady reached the place. While I was standing there doing nothing, she asked me to help an elderly acquaintance of her down the steps. This sounded a bit rude to me. But I still helped as I won't utter harsh words to people. Needless to say, the woman who said this to me was very rich, but very prayerful.

Mother, though she is too prayerful, has never showed such attitude to me. She never speaks out of the blue and asks me to offer my seat to the elderly person standing next to you in the church. Even though I'm very young enough to expect this.

2. I'm your mother; get this thing done for me

I've met many such people. Many of them are women. They show an attitude that can be termed as overly demanding dignity. It is mainly out of place and not needed.

Recently, I was traveling in an intra city bus. The bus was crowded and as is the norm in our city, the ladies have a seating area at the front part of the bus. An overly demanding dignity woman was seated at the rear of the bus which everybody here assumes as the men's seating area.

So, I was waiting to occupy this woman's seat after she

alights at her stop. When her turn came to alight, to my inconvenience, this woman showed me the hand and this attitude so that a person of her choice—maybe her acquaintance—can be seated in her place instead of me.

As can be understood, I could have ignored her attitude and occupied the seat because nothing could have stopped me- just the hand. I thought it would be rude on my part towards her and I did nothing like that. Justified or not, nonetheless she was rude.

So, these are the ways that people offend others daily as this woman did during my bus commute.

Another time, I was with my dad getting my passport done at a government office. There were a few stages to complete this documentation and have the cherished document in my hand.

As the queue for the issuance of the passport progressed to a stage wherein a photocopy of some of our batch of candidates' documents was needed, a woman with this above attitude cropped up. She jumped the queue and asked a man waiting for his turn with a blatant gesture of handing over her document to get the photocopy done.

He could have refused. But with the overly demanding dignity of this woman, the man obliged and she got the photocopy well ahead of others who were waiting for their turn in the queue.

Such a demeanour is rather unsettling and can be threatening too.

Nonetheless, Mother has never shown such kind of attitude towards me. It is never in her nature to do it. She rather has a pleasant tone when she wants to get things done for her. This warm and gentler undertone is quite a comforting one too. As I said earlier, she is from heaven and this place is very cherished to enter into with no 'lording over' or 'overly demanding dignity' looks.

3. Give alms to that beggar

During many instances, I have passed by a beggar and did not give him any alms. This may be because I was rather childish and silly. I had many thoughts running in my mind: naivety; the alms not being put to good use by the beggar but to get drunk; a gang operating that utilizes the alms.

Naivety being that I would be very self-aware of what would people say if I would just make a stop on my way to somewhere and tended to a beggar or gave them alms. I was of the opinion that people would mistake me for a silly, diffident and awkward person. These were exactly my thoughts and I don't know if it would make sense to anyone reading this.

All this aside, there was not even one instance of Mother admonishing me to give alms to these beggars. She never said that they are in dire need of it and it is a sin to ignore them. This is because she knows my heart. It is very special and rare as she has said multiple times.

Conclusion

Attitude is not needed in a perfect society. When such defensive norms are let go, people can live far better and thrive holistically. This is what heaven is- a perfect society and a far better world [Mt 6:19]. This is from where Mother is and the very thing is reflected in her talks or mannerisms. What remains is a memory to be long cherished, which, otherwise, would be a bitter experience with such erring and demanding people around.

CHAPTER FIVE

No Affirmation

There is this practice in people we meet in our everyday life that they affirm their stance or position on the various topics they talk to us. It is to lay credence to the statements they are making in these conversations. It may range from a simple, 'I know him for 9 years' to 'I have an experience in the said field for twelve years'. This list can go on and on. If they do not use these statements of affirmations, maybe people won't believe them.

Mother has never asserted using such statements while she has talked to me.

Typical statements

1. Trust me; I'm a mother
2. I know your father since eternity; I rule in heaven
3. I'm a writer; I have an experience of 10 years

Explanations

1. Trust me; I'm a mother

In almost more than ten years she has talked to me, Mother has never made this statement. She gently and playfully gives in and joins my conversation on silly topics. They may range from her comforting me to gleefully playing with me.

Many times, as many parents do, she says, 'I'm a mother'. But she rarely uses the above statement with the prefix, 'Trust me' or 'Believe me'.

This behaviour is very in-line with her reputation of being caring and gentle. She's never assertive to sound superior or authoritative.

2. I know your father since eternity; He was not so; I rule in heaven

There have never been such statements coming from Mother. When I ponder over many earthly and heavenly mysteries like how could she have talked to Jesus or whether he possessed many good virtues since a very young age.

Once I asked her about our Lord's conduct with her. She said that he was very obedient. But never made the above statement tersely that she knew him for so many years and obviously he would be good to her. Also, not that they both rule in heaven since eternity. In all convenience, she could have made such statements. But she doesn't choose to.

She is very proud of him too, as he is the fruit of her womb that has made her so blessed with just a yes to the message from St Gabriel [Psalm 127:3].

3. I'm a writer; I have an experience of 10 years

These are often the typical statements we make during our conversations with colleagues and juniors at our workplace. This is to assert our infallible authority regarding the various challenges faced at the office or our advice that the juniors need to take in office matters. Needless to say, more the experience, more is the weight attached to the statement.

But Mother need not make such dainty statements as I'm centuries older than you or so. It's because I love her very much from the heart and being bound in love, there doesn't come any possibility of me not believing her talks. It is always a very remote possibility.

Conclusion

The thought that we need to make assertions to make ourselves heard and felt in the crowd of highly talented people is just a response from our ego. We need not make these if governed by pure emotions and feelings towards the person we talk to. In my case, it works out between me and Mother as I respect her authority of being Our Lady.

And out of a child's love towards her too. In response towards my talks with her that she is My Lady, she does get embarrassed and genuinely so. But out of the depths of her heart she says that she is a mother first and I comply with her. She has always shown herself to be a mother with me and I can't deny that.

Mother was always available at hand whenever disaster struck for me. Maybe in the case of demonic possession I experienced as recorded in my life journey or other cases, she always helped zealously. She is indeed an ideal and perfect mother- a treasure to have in one's life.

No Accusation

It is a common norm to see everywhere around that people lose patience and bring all sorts of accusations against each other, may they be family members too. Mother is not so. She shows a lot of enduring patience.

To enumerate one such instance, I was prayerless for quite a period of a decade and the powers of darkness took over my life. They were everywhere around wreaking a kind of havoc. I was oblivious to this and she could not help me as I never gave her or God enough power through my daily fervent prayers—amounting to hours—that I do now.

In spite of all these abominable activities of demons in my life, she and God never budged, showing utmost patience. I can only imagine if coming face-to-face with such a situation, there would be numerous instances of me losing patience- being angry, annoyed and miffed. This I do every time when trying to convince my family members to pray more so that many problems in our lives could be solved. To be precise, there are more benefits in my life too if they started praying constantly and vociferously. After all, the whole family suffers when only few people pray in it.

Coming to the point, she and God used to constantly talk to me through many of the preachers and prayerful people around to start praying. The idea sounded impossible to me. But at the opportune moment Mother intervened as I have mentioned in the previous pages about my life's journey.

Her patience all through was admirable. Though I would say she didn't bring scandalous accusations, there were instances like, 'nothing can happen if you don't pray' or 'I pray to God to take away idleness in you' heard from many preachers who came to pray at our house or when I visited prayer centres; there were always gentle exhortations.

Praying is always the bone of contention between God and Satan.

Mother has never leveled against me demeaning or destructive accusations. And this is because she is not human and full of grace to not do so [Luke 1:28].

Typical statements

1. You are mortal and weak to do that
2. You commit this mistake or sin again and again
3. You are known to do this
4. Eat less. You always eat above the limit.
5. You have no gratitude

Explanations

1. You are mortal

Mother doesn't accuse me of being a mortal and thus she finds many weaknesses in me. Though a number of times I have shown my weakness through being emotionally charged as I had my brother or cousin visiting me, she has never done this.

To elaborate further, I have not found the inclination to pray my usual prayers when my brother was visiting from abroad or any relatives come visiting. Being emotionally involved in spending time with them and not finding time to meditate on the scriptures was often the case. This was so because meditating on the scriptures requires a lonely place and lot of silence around.

With my kin's company, this wouldn't be possible as there would be a lot of noise, talking and me getting involved in the conversation as they demand a response all the time, expecting me to interact.

Mother never said that I'm human and do all this in a demeaning way. But she was silent all the time these events were unfolding. She would talk in words like, 'I'll help you' when I was anxious because I had not prayed the usual prayers and the forces of darkness would take advantage.

But during the next prayer, she would anxiously say, 'I was waiting'.

2. You're a habitual sinner

It's our human tendency to get frustrated easily. Also, it is again our human tendency to commit the same mistake or sin again and again- maybe in many cases without remorse. We are not conscious and even the context or circumstance repeating over and over again, plays spoilsport.

She never made this statement to me and never tried to hide her displeasure at being offended by me again and again; she wasn't displeased in the first place. It is natural to her. And because she is heavenly, there is no room for altercation or miff or annoyance, even discreetly. It is natural to her and that is how she is.

3. You are known to do this

When we look around, there are many cases wherein we see people making accusations against the younger ones. Looking at these little ones' parents, people compare them with their lineage or parents or even kin and relatives. They say that this child is the way he is because his parents were so; his brothers are so; his mother was so. Such people get even more accusing and say the little one resembles them in every way. And I'm talking here about vices and bad habits; not about looks or good behaviour.

I have come across many such instances of people accusing the younger ones. A known person to me was drinking alcohol and was found sometimes in an inebriated condition in the streets. Because his father was doing the same in his younger days, the kin around began saying, 'he does it because his father was doing the same'. Otherwise, the guy is quite studious and intelligent.

While in many cases this may be partly true, but children have their own identity. The little ones should be welcomed and encouraged to live a holy life resembling Christ and not any one not worth resembling.

That being said, Mother has never said this about me. Though I come from a good family, people can still find reasons to accuse me may be because of the hometown I belong to or the larger community I represent.

Actually, my hometown is known to have had some quite harrowing accusations made against them. It is of accusing a great man of God about swindling finances of the Church and threatening him with lathis or cudgels. There are many incidents like this. This being said, the man was very holy and an exemplary priest by name, Fr Agnelo de Souza; he is at the moment declared Venerable by the Church.

To update on the same, while I was praying, I felt the presence of Fr Agnel for a good 40 minutes. Mother said he has forgiven the same transgression against him and no offense remained with him for the above incidents in our hometown. As he was a beloved servant of God, these former things displeased him greatly. And the same is like a blemish on our hometown for long, say close to a century.

The history never made Mother to accuse me that I

belong to this hometown. And she never gave in to this thought that I am sometimes lax at prayer because of this. This is so as one accusation in your mind leads to another and goes on and on. It has a cascading effect on your mind and can have a devastating effect on the person's demeanour.

Mother is not so. She says that I'm a very special and great man of God. There is no one like me in the whole world and very unique. Also, I'm very pleasing to God.

"This is my beloved son, in whom I am well pleased."
Matthew 3:17 KJV

Mother has also said that I will bring honour to my motherland or hometown because of the manner of my death and the place where it will happen making up for the above blemish. I know every bit of tiny detail about this event that is to take place: the time; day; year. I saw a heavenly calendar that revealed this date in a vision. It said 17 EPO 1019 and will be my feast day.

There is nothing to be scared of about this event as there are ample testimonies in the bible with glaring statements and references.

"O death, where is thy sting?"
1Corinthians 15:55 KJV

The Saints knew the exact moment and manner of their death. And still, it didn't bother or weary them. One of them was St Edith Stein. As is obvious, she died in a gas chamber during the holocaust.

To elucidate on the same, the victims during their final moments left scratch marks from their nails on the ceiling of these gas chambers; this death was that harrowing. But she wasn't deterred by the thought of it and the death was always played before her in the visions that she saw about it. The precious blood of Jesus is the courage of martyrs.

4. Eat less. You always eat above the limit

As there is demonic interference in my life because I bring resistance to their kingdom in the God's good world, Mother has asked me to eat less since about a decade. Deliverance works through fasting as many demons won't leave unless one fasts and prays.

Mother said that I should not fast with rigour as many holy people of God do. Instead, she has asked me to eat in moderate quantities- not to stomach full. This helps her in combating evil influences in and around me.

The reason for this request from her is that I am just an infant in the spirit. And, as anyone can tell, parents don't find it pleasing if their infant goes without food for its stomach. They just don't like it and feel for them.

Also, I won't stand this strict rigour of fasting and this is the same reason Mother has not called me to the religious life, although many great Saints can be found to be throughout history.

Actually, many sisters of a particular congregation

approached me to come and join their community which is at a two-hour distance from my home. This they did after finding out that I was very prayerful and always reciting prayers at our parish church they frequented.

I revealed to them that Mother has inspired me in prayers to be a lay preacher in some time to serve God. Later, they stopped coaxing.

Coming to the point, there are innumerable times in this combat between God and Satan, where I end up eating a bit more than the prescribed moderate quantity. This means the power of evil influence increases in me and there is resistance to God's good work; it may be prayer too.

When this happens, Mother has never accused me of being irresponsible or nonconforming to her request. She just says with concern that she will help me or she is with me. This is not my fault when I eat more, but I'm compelled to through demonic influence when I mock certain spirits. It is a common occurrence that whenever we are in contact with someone powerful enough to harm us in any way, there are ample chances of us mocking them.

It may be like talking about their inability to work more in our lives because of God being in control or them tormenting us above our tolerance limit and many other ways. Also, it may be telling them that God can bring down their stronghold. Although God is more powerful than anyone, there are times when he works and the spirits are in control.

The deliverance from God is an ongoing thing and a constant struggle. He has to wrest us out from the demonic clutches. For some it is a very long spiritual battle. But for someone so precious to him like me, God can do wonders as and when he pleases.

5. You have no gratitude

This kind of statement comes in every talk between parents and children. Erring children who talk against and have a kind of negative attitude towards their parents get such responses from them.

Sometimes, this kind of verbal reaction from the parents comes from a deep sense of ingratitude felt by them from their kids. They hold fast to the thought that they have nurtured their kids in every way and helped them grow with the best kind of upbringing possible.

During some dire situations, they may have sacrificed a lot. It may even be begging for money from relatives and friends to fend for their children's career or getting some loan at very high interest rates to further their schooling.

Parents can do such things that require insurmountable hardships and sacrifices. But these earthly parents keep harping the same old melody of ingratitude. Maybe they do this because they are human. And we know that everybody around is.

But Mother has never made this statement ever to me though she has given me everything through her intercession. This is because she is too good and gentle to even think about it. And also, since I am a good child, there never comes a situation where such talks can be resulted in conversation with my earthly parents too.

But Mother is very accommodating. Talking to her is my best pastime; she is a breeze to be with.

Conclusion

Accusations are not Mother's style of dealing with her beloved ones. We know who is the one who accuses our brothers and sisters day and night [Revelation 12:10]. God has plans for everyone and it does not work by threatening or coaxing. This is done by the Devil and she does not take part in it in any way.

Her way is that which leads to Jesus Christ. And he himself is known to be Prince of Peace professing all the time the need to love one another. It is the greatest commandment: love one another and love God [Matthew 22:37–40].

Love is God's persona [John 3:16] and Mother is the same- gentle and loving.

CHAPTER SEVEN

No Harsh Tone

It is a human tendency to reply in a harsh tone to people-may be to prove their point or in irritation. This is a very rude thing to do to people and is not practised in heaven. There is nothing rude prevalent there. Also, as Mother is from heaven, she doesn't do this to me, come what may.

I have never seen her doing this for any reason. There are numerous instances where she could have done this. Maybe when I was silly too, but she patiently listens to everything. More of this in the later chapters.

All she does is being calm, gentle and concerned. She does reply in these tones all the time.

Typical statements

1. You are grounded
2. Don't keep mocking him
3. You didn't give alms. That needy person is suffering from a week.

Explanations

1. You are grounded

Many people have professed in my life about me being a very good son and child. One of these was a close acquaintance of mine whom I met at my parish church. She used to work there as a sacristan, though not for the pay.

Once during a casual conversation after the mass between a nun, my mother and this sacristan, this lady remarked to my mother that there is no one like her son i.e., me in the whole world. She further stated that if I would have been tiny and not 5'9", she would have carried me in her arms and taken me everywhere.

This sacristan considered me as her child and the nun—joining in the conversation through inspiration from God—pointed out to me that I should be happy that I have two mothers. This was because I used to be very sad in my looks during that time as it was the time when I was possessed by the demon, though quite discreetly.

Also, during my early adolescent days, I started working at a place near my house. The girls there—because of my naivety and innocence they got to know through my talks—started teasing me; it was a daily affair.

While one girl was at it, a lady said to her that I am not from here or this place- as roughly translated. She meant to say that I'm from heaven and this is the reason that I'm so innocent to the evils prevalent in the world- totally preserved from it. Everyone there believed me to be so.

So being such a very good child, Mother has never used the phrase of 'you are grounded' against me. She keeps telling me that I'm a very good and holy child; there is no one like me in this whole world. This is the statement oft repeated by many people I have met in my life. And Mother repeats it too.

2. Don't keep mocking him

As I said, there has been a spiritual battle against me all my life and it is raging with some agents of Satan set against me with specific missions to accomplish. To counter them, I need to pray daily and eat moderately, always being guided by Mother and God.

While Jesus shows urgency in his talks always to pray and asks me to be clothed in power to tackle the wily darts of the enemy as Satan is always ready to use me, 'he's waiting', Mother is different. She is shown to me in visions with concern, bending forward and talking as one does to a child with all her royal robes.

I keep mocking these agents of Satan all the time. It may be out of frustration or a nagging psychological tendency to do it all the time; I still don't know the reason. But Mother says that I'm not like that and the last person to court trouble or instigate a fight. Of this, though, I am sure.

When I do this, she keeps telling me gently with concern—and not with harsh tones—to stop mocking him.

The aftermath of the mocking is always met with Mother saying gently that I mocked him. I am aware of this fact and to be sure, she makes me vigilant too.

But there is not much danger to me from these evil attacks, as I'm predestined. God works in me even amidst this. He's totally composed and prepared, leading me into the predestined things he has prepared through my daily dose of prayer.

Also, the torture as an aftermath of this mocking of mine is very mild because of God's graces abounding in me. And to add another point, though the demon may take me into his vile ways and torture for a few days, maybe, because of his power, I get reverted back to my praying ways or the course predestined for me by God right away; this is always the case as my Father doesn't want to lose me, come what may.

"You prepare a table before me in the presence of my enemies;
You anoint my head with oil; my cup overflows."
Psalm 23:5 NRSVCE

"I will go before you and level the mountains,
I will break in pieces the doors of bronze
And cut through the bars of iron"
Isaiah 45:2 NRSVCE

"Behold, I have set before you an open door,
That no man can shut"
Revelation 3:8 NRSVCE

The door of heaven is always open before me.

3. You didn't give alms

There are many instances wherein I have passed by beggars who frequent my commonly visited roads. They seem to beg intently so as to pass the hurdles for the day of obtaining food for their stomach. Many times, I don't have enough lesser denomination notes to give them in alms. But it is my practice to give them food to eat from the restaurants I know rather than money as many are known to get drunk and pass out on the streets.

Though Mother perceives that the beggar has a great need of the money I give in alms and still I don't intend to do so, she doesn't for a wee bit consider admonishing me for not helping these poor souls.

Never has she given angry looks too saying, 'You didn't give alms'. But I manage sometimes somehow to give these underprivileged people any food or lesser denomination currency notes regularly. It is a good practice.

My dad used to do the same and nobody ever knew how big an amount of money he has donated in charity; all the guesses were inaccurate given to his status in society. Charity has to be done so; nobody should know [Matthew 6:3].

Conclusion

Mother never speaks to me rudely nor is there ever a rude reply to anything I ask. As already discussed, she has an exhortative attitude with many caring words. I cannot even imagine what all I have learnt from being always in the company of this loving mother. She is a role model for everyone- even great Saints.

These holy people were known to be very close to her. As she speaks to me constantly, all the time, it has left a lasting impact on me. As they say, 'good company reflects on your persona'. I'm truly blessed to have her in me.

CHAPTER EIGHT

No Rude Behaviour/ Angry Looks

There are ample instances in our daily dealing with people in the world wherein they give angry looks if their repeated attempts to exhort a given thing from us have failed. They get annoyed and frustrated easily, using other means to get the same thing done. It may be through angry looks or threatening, whichever they feel is tangible. And yes, things get going and some breakthroughs appear if this is done.

But this is not Mother's style of working. She waits and waits until things start to work by God's grace.

Typical statements

1. Stay inside. Covid is looming large
2. Get working

Explanations

1. Stay inside. Covid is looming large

Mother has helped me greatly during the ongoing pandemic. Many had lost their lives in our country. There were four or five relatives of mine too who succumbed to the second wave of the deadly pestilence.

But there were many instances wherein Mother helped me greatly. She answered my prayers of getting the vaccinations immediately near my place. I did not want to travel to far places as it was risky and one could catch the infection easily.

The first instance was that a camp was organized by an NGO near our place- some 50 feet from our house. I just had to walk near to the place and got myself vaccinated. But for my family members this was not the case as they panicked and rushed to reputed hospitals to get vaccinated. I just blindly believed that Mother would help.

The second instance was wherein a neighbour took me to a nearby primary health care centre and after getting me the vaccination, dropped me back home. Getting all of these doses was very convenient and I still remember Mother's help for me not having to spend even a single dime.

The third instance was that two government hospital nurses came calling to our door to come and get the vaccination under a tree, just some 80 feet from my home. I just went there and got vaccinated. There was no queue at all.

All this was possible through Mother's intercession.

But during this deadly, horrifying period of eerie feeling around, when I ventured outside with my close friends and family to enjoy leisurely time from work or get some fresh air, Mother never asked me in dictating terms or angry looks to stay inside.

She is with me whatever I do and endorses me in everything. Isn't this how mothers are to their very good and trustworthy children? In all possibilities, they are.

2. Get working

I procrastinate sometimes, though rarely. But these episodes could be because of a spiritual attack and they can be nagging. But, as I said, God still works because of my predestination to heaven.

It is regarding this book. I had just finished writing three books and one was on the way to be published. It is a collection of 60 essays like the first one with ample anecdotes about the Saints. And I have won an award for the second published book *The Body Language Trail* with a noted secular publisher.

So, after a few months since publishing this second book of mine, out of the blue, Mother spoke to me that I will write another book shortly. I understood what this meant. This was the same for the second book and after this revelation from Mother, I started writing that book *The*

Body Language Trail in five days.

I thoroughly enjoyed writing it with ample anecdotes from my life wherein all the incidents that inspired a particular body language nonverbal cue was shared. And I finished it in ten days or so.

I surmised that the same would happen in the case of this book too. Being elated for a while, I totally forgot about the revelation from Mother and got about doing my own business without a knowledge about the same.

Then, after five days, while I was returning from my daily mass routine from the parish church, she started talking about the new about-to-be-written book again.

This time, I felt inspired with plenty of content and jotted it down after returning home on a notepad. The list became very long and I thought that it is enough material to write the book Mother had stated about.

The book you are reading is the one about *What Our Lady Sounds Like?* that was planned by Mother for me to write.

I doubted about it a lot that whether it would be enough content to put forth in a book. And more impetus was provided to me by Mother from my conversations with a fellow parishioner.

So, I had shelved this project more than two times to look into it at a later stage as and when I get inspired to write more content for the same. But Mother never spoke to me, as in office circles, 'You should be working' or 'Don't be lazy' or 'hustle'.

This is not how she is. But is always praying and I have visions of her rather vaguely of holding a rosary and saying with concern, 'write' or 'write about it'; I have never seen her in full majesty, ever. Rather, every word like this I just shared is full of concern and prayerful wishes.

Maybe, me writing this book was predestined too. But it is spectacular to watch God working in mysterious ways. He is totally cool and a person worthy of emulating. We are called to be imitators of Christ [Ephesians 5:1].

Conclusion

Mother never can express herself rudely so as to cause harm or bring about some negative emotions in people. But she can do only so in the presence of evil. As she did in my life incident on the social medium to that admin and other people in the group from her tutelage.

She says that her rude talks are not for me and even hell is not for me. Hence, I should not mention about it.

Mother loves talking to me and has a pet name for me. She has never talked rudely or scolded me for anything. I'm her pet child always pleasing her in everything I do. Everything about me pleases her. And I think I'm overwhelmed, happy too to hear about this. God willed it to be so.

CHAPTER NINE

No Abrasive Talk

People we meet make mildly abrasive talks to admonish someone being nosy or ward off silliness from a person they are in a conversation with. This is the common norm and the reaction may be because of annoyance or just sheer perplexity that someone can even reply as such with total naivety and innocence.

My mother does that all the time. Whenever I'm near a television set, many such silly responses crop up as I watch television only passively or to say, when someone turns the set on. It is never me switching on the television.

One such incident is when cricket is played live. She always confuses the highlights or replay of the boundary hit by the cricketer during live television with a new ball hit for a boundary. It is always confusing for her and she can't make out the difference.

I do get annoyed and reply in a mildly stern voice that it is not a new ball but an old ball that the cricketer has hit for a boundary.

Mother has never been like this to me. I do this to my

mother but love her very much. Maybe Mother has never done this to me because she loves me more than I love my earthly mother.

Typical statements

1. Don't be silly
2. I have taught that to you

Explanations

1. Don't be silly

I can come across as silly, particularly with Mother as she notices me and is with me all the time. This could be in numerous instances that can happen in everybody's life. But it can't be limited to one. Truly I am silly most of the times. But she is not in any sense.

This was particularly during my office commuting days. I used to travel in buses with daily passes. It was a long journey of one and a half hour to travel from my home to the workplace and pretty arduous, as I may recall it. But I love traveling in buses. It is pleasurable for me.

As the bus would set forth on its journey, I would get impatient and anxious of commuters getting in and out of it at various terminals. The thought that when I reach my destination alighting from the bus would be a hassle and I won't be heard by the conductor to stop at the required terminal, would always bug me.

This would be constant headache and as it was a peak

hour of people commuting to their workplace, it would get on my nerves. But still I managed by God's grace.

May be this is silly, but this was how I was.

Another instance is when Mother asked me to attend the fellowship of a ministry that I came to know through my relatives. It is a very good place but quite far from my home.

She used to ask me constantly for quite a time to attend it every week as it was good for me to get delivered from satanic strongholds and such. But I was worrying about how to meet the people or ministers there and how to find the bus route leading to the place. It was very daunting to me.

This may be labeled as shyness and introversion. But I was thus, completely different from what I am now. It has been a complete transformative journey in my life as everyone who know me and around my neighbourhood know. They notice God's hand in this entirely and have great reverence for me.

Though I was silly during this period and very rarely now, I was never wimpy. I never lacked the courage to suffer for God and his plans, making great sacrifices and even greater risks to achieve the same. As someone said, 'spirituality is not for wimps'. It is true. The Saints were very courageous.

I also lacked the gumption to do many tasks. But, anyways, managed to do them all the time through God's grace.

Mother has never admonished me because I'm silly with her or anyone else. She perceives a very loving, good, trustworthy child in me who dares to love her and God with anything that comes across, never budging down. I'm used to get things done the hard way. In other words, psychologically very strong.

2. I taught that to you

There have been numerous instances wherein Mother could have replied with this statement. But she does not. In fact, she has taught me numerous things and has never credited herself to have done it.

God is thus too. He works every great quality in people and praises them to have it in them- be it valour of kings/armies [Jeremiah 6:22–25] or good qualities of holy people like Nathanael [John 1:47]. But, as is understood, he gives them the grace. And yet, doesn't acknowledge it because—in a way—it is his work that is showing up in them or everywhere. He doesn't take direct credit. Instead praises his creation.

Everything on earth is his. And I take it this way that my life too is his. Going by this logic, he can do anything that he wants with my life. I will not complain and he does not require permission to do the same; I never ask him to. But he says that he doesn't intend life to be this way.

Mother too is of the same opinion. She says that I'm not a thing to be used but a person with a free will.

Taking credit has never been hers or God's way. In fact, he is creditworthy.

She has blessed me with intellectual abilities that involve a highfalutin vocabulary with a complex mind. Also, ability to understand body language of people just by looking at their mannerisms and gestures. I used to observe and learn.

Each time I learnt them through incidents mentioned in the book *The Body Language Trail* she used to say that I will learn even many more of them. So, they are in my arsenal and I use them to analyze people in everyday dealings.

There are many such creditworthy instances wherein she has blessed me and never taken credit for it or said the above line.

This instance was wherein she showed me how society works when I was being cornered and used by people around because of my naivety or innocence. She asked me to be with friends and learn the behaviour of the whole bunch of people.

Mother gave quite an outline as to how the various strata of people behave. She showed that people in authority or quite a status like me of being a writer dress themselves very well and are presentable. And even professionals skilled in a particular trade dress as such to show allegiance to it. Otherwise, as she concurred, people won't respect me.

Not to sound disobedient to her, I obeyed and my whole life changed with people calling me with the title, 'Sir'.

More so, she also showed me other things like people of my age i.e., youth, do not roam around with their parents; carry office items in tote bags, but in knapsacks; behave in a way with those around. She revealed that else the youth won't respect me.

Also, some people in the unit of society talk about the weather around; ask about each other's well-being; enquire about them having had food. Any talks deviating from this, they won't take me seriously and label me as a child. This I am, but they take it in a derogatory and less creditworthy way.

There is more to it. She helped me be strong and prove my mettle against a wily person. Mother revealed that I should not: ask him questions; linger around him while he is talking about his profession and workplace matters; be silly; show concern like asking about his family, friends. I did this and won respect from this person.

She asked me to do this until he respected me. After that I should stop doing this.

My neighbours are less privileged and mother used to help them with ration or money. Soon they started expecting more and tormenting my mother with politics, envy, greed, denying favours, among other things.

Mother revealed to me that she should maintain a level of

dignity with these people around. She should not mingle with them unnecessarily and remain aloof; speak in a stern way. Soon, this problem vanished and there was peace around.

Mother is very wise and I have encountered her wisdom firsthand. There is no one I met wiser than her as she is rightly called 'The seat of wisdom'. Or in other terms, wisdom rests on her.

This being said, she doesn't command credit for helping me with all this. But Mother asks me to give glory to God in everything. She is no stranger to this fact that her whole life was a pleasing sacrifice to God. Being called to serve eternally having the Saints in her courts, the title of 'Queen of angels and Saints' rightly suits her.

Conclusion

Mother loves me very much. Even if I'm silly she finds me cute and is pleased always. This means to say that she finds my cuteness all the time- be it in talks or gestures. As she is greatly pleased with me, talking to me in abrasive terms is the last thing Mother will do. And also, she is not known to react as such. It does not behove of her.

There have never been such conversations of mine with her wherein she appeared to be annoyed or under stress dealing with me as parents always do with children. I think it is safe to say that if people talk to me for a few minutes, their stress completely vanishes into thin air.

I am totally grateful to God for giving me such a life, being loved by everyone around and especially, dear Mother. He has satisfied me fully and is continuing to do so even now. It is under progress.

"I would feed you with the finest of wheat, and with Honey from the rock I would satisfy you."
Psalm 81:16 NRSVCE

CHAPTER TEN

No Comparison

Earthly parents often compare their children with their peers. Also, some competitive peers compare themselves with their counterparts so that they may stay abreast of the cut-throat competition around in the society. This comparison—among adults—is mostly about money and position with some covetousness regarding goods too. It is an unhealthy competition and brings about envy and hatred.

Also, such kind of competition is not from God and most of them are a violation of God's commandments. But nonetheless, this is the norm everywhere.

Coming to the behaviour of parents regarding their children, it is also an unhealthy and unconducive comparison pertaining to the child's success or goals. Goals need to be set. But no two children are the same.

As you can see, when they grow up, they each have different designations at workplace; status in society; dissimilar professions and more. Some children may have become successful in later part of their life or age as me. Others might have chosen career paths that are totally different and unique.

Passions must be cultivated at a young age, but they keep changing over the course of time. The right and buoyant passion should help a child to be successful in life later on. What parents can do is give them an education up till master's and let the child decide the course of its future dreams.

Mother never compared me as such with anyone around. My earthly mother never did too. In fact, as I was a bright student during my early days, people around asked their children to be like me.

As I am totally consecrated to God, Mother is pleased with my every word or action. I am always working for her.

Typical statements

1. You could have done better than your colleague
2. My son was not like this
3. Learn from your brother
4. Be like your mother

Explanations

1. You could have done better than your colleague

There were many colleagues at my workplace that I managed to get into in the later part of my life. They were having degrees to fend for. But I was lacking them when compared. Mother never asked me to get some like them and be more professional. She knows what's good for me.

For now, I do freelance writing and have a few clients. I know she imagined this future for me.

But, to elaborate further, I never was underestimated at my workplace. All the colleagues there held me in high regard because of my intellectual prowess. I used to produce articles for complex topics. Most of them who admired me at my workplace were software engineers- close to 30 of them; I was a star performer.

2. My son was not like this

As we all know, Jesus Christ was the epitome of holiness during his earthly life too [Revelation 5:1–5]. There was no sin that anybody around could accuse him of [John 8:46a]. He dared the Jews with this question. But they brought inane accusations against him that he has a demon.

Being the mother of such a pure and holy God-himself-made-man, she could accuse anybody of not conforming to the standards of him. But she does not do so because if she starts accusing, nobody would remain as all have sinned and fallen short of the glory of God [Romans 3:23].

Nonetheless, she loving prods us to be like him and follow his example- the blessed fruit of her womb. Maybe she knows it is unhealthy to compare and she has never made this statement while engaging in conversation with me.

3. Learn from your brother

My brother started working at a young age shelving his dreams of completing a post-graduation degree. I did not start working formally till quite a few years in the foreground. But even my earthly mother is an ideal woman and kept my formal clothes neatly ironed in the wardrobe in the hopes that I would join a workplace someday.

Mothers are firm believers. And like my earthly mother, my heavenly Mother too doesn't compare me with anyone in God's whole wide world. My mother maybe sad upon hearing news of my old batchmates doing well quite some time ago, still never compared me with them too.

Coming to my brother's issue, Mother never said this word in all these years she has spoken to me. She never asked me to become more responsible and mature like him taking care of the family. Maybe because she knew what future she was holding for me in the years ahead.

All the more, she is always aware that I'm working for her and was during this time too. She is well-pleased and is very proud of me.

4. Be like your mother

I'm always troubled in my emotions due to certain bondages. They keep playing about in my head and I won't have inclination to do certain things. Household chores is not my thing. My mother keeps doing them all the time and she is tired during most part of the day.

She keeps asking me to do some thing or the other like cleaning cobwebs or dusting the vase and showpieces. But I keep neglecting it for the same reason as stated above.

Mother being a silent spectator to all this at home, has never asked me to be diligent and hardworking like my earthly mother. She has never dictated to me in strict terms that I should help her with my young blood.

She's like that and knows people inside out. And it is perfect enough to judge people.

Conclusion

Mother never fosters envy in the mind of her loved ones. This competition around can be labeled as disguised envy. Material goods do not keep people happy but a close companionship with God. He created us and our hearts won't rest until they find him. Christ intended himself to be the king of our hearts.

His mother can lead us on this earth to satisfy us fully just as he does. Sometimes they work in tandem- he and her. He's speaking through her mostly.

It is delightful to be in the loving eyes and care of Mother. She desires us to be full of possessions in heaven where moth and rust do not destroy [Matthew 6:19–20]. We have a loving mother who understands our needs fully.

CHAPTER ELEVEN

No Blame

Whenever people are in some or the other situation together, they blame each other if things go wrong. The fact that the other person seemed like was not doing the best to help them out, keeps nagging them all the time. Also, if someone wants to bring you out of a situation and finds you seemingly less cooperating to get out of the muck, words blaming the victim come into play.

Friends are used to do this. One of my friends who was a batchmate in my college used to help me with everything. He was close to my parents and constantly helping with things around even to get my used books to deliver to my place. This was 35 Km from his house.

When my parents enquired him about why my performance was so dismal in the examinations, he retorted that I am a very lazy person. But it was not so. In fact, there were many other connected reasons working discreetly; I just could not concentrate.

My friend felt that he was left out in me not being cooperative with his efforts to excel academically.

Mother has brought me out of many situations that I

faced in my life- most of them dire. But she has never complained or blamed me for not being up to the mark with the things she asked me to do.

She can never do it and it is not her character too.

Typical statements

1. Your prayerlessness has brought you to this state
2. Cry and pray; your prayers are not effective

Explanations

1. Your prayerlessness has brought you to this state

As I said, the blame can take any shape and magnitude. I was prayerless for most part of my life and through this laxity, I became entangled in many bondages. Some were of very serious nature and others were not so.

Mother delivered me from the serious pangs of demonic possessions. But the milder ones are in her elaborate plans for me to bring good out of them [Romans 8:28]. As it can be said, God works through her amidst this. It is his plans that she brings out; we both serve the same God.

But though things got difficult for me during this whole deliverance fiasco, Mother was very composed. Maybe she supplies me with graces instead of talking or blaming.

There were many times wherein demons used to make me run from pillar to post or going round in circles with no result. They would operate by interfering in work. I would be confused and forgetting things, the plot or topics in question pertaining to my content writing job for hours together. Some tasks that could be completed in ten minutes would take hours together.

Still, Mother never used to panic and there was not even a wee bit of wavering in her voice. Her stance is buoyant. Mother is thus.

She never made this above statement and I think that makes her very cool to be sought after to be friends with.

2. Cry and pray; your prayers are not effective

Since my deliverance from the first demonic possession, I was praying all day long. It was rosaries for me all the time since Mother showed me their power in the spiritual realm through this deliverance. I was seeking for more powerful prayers and had asked Mother in my conversations with her since the time. This prayer was answered very unexpectedly when I had not thought that it would be granted.

As I was sitting in the fifth pew in our parish church before the blessed sacrament, the difficulty was dealt with. Praying thus was my routine during those days. I would go to the church well before the onset of evening and pray the rosaries for 2–3 hours. They were my staple diet for the day; in a day I would say 18 of these.

When I started praying the remainder of the rosaries for the day, an elderly lady from the first pew of the church before the blessed sacrament stood and was about to leave. When she was passing by me in the fifth pew, she stood near me. Using both her hands, humbly, she gave me a booklet containing these powerful prayers compiled by a renowned priest-cum-preacher who conducts prayer at a retreat centre in our city.

Offering them, she said 'Son' and I accepted that booklet from her. I knew right away that it was an answer to my prayers when in conversation with Mother regarding the same. And these prayers helped me to be more prepared with graces for my journey to complete deliverance.

Mother can answer any prayer and she is mindful of me even when I talk about some difficulty during my casual conversation with her. This incident is a good reminder of the same.

She has never said that my prayers are not effective and I'm not praying from my heart or so. But Mother has helped me to pray effective prayers as those above. She works as such. Instead of talking, she acts.

Whatever bad may have happened in our life as it did with my prayerlessness since a long time, Mother does not blame us for not being vigilant. But she considers what needs to be done so that we can come out of it.

Blaming, as we can see in her ways, does not solve any problem. We just have to look for the remedy. She's always looking for it through her great wisdom and has helped me through many difficulties I faced in life.

Conclusion

The attitude of Mother wherein she never blames me for my weaknesses or frailties can be understood by meditating on her concern for me. She is concerned for my well-being and this overrides the need to focus on blaming. Mother has a very special place for me in her heart. The fact that her heart burns with love for me amid all the difficulties I get into or have faced throughout my life helps me be at peace, rest assured.

A mother who is perfect like her is a very good thing to cherish. I am truly blessed!

CHAPTER TWELVE

Not Rudely Cautious

It is true people can get rudely cautious if they encounter something out of the blue, when least expected. This encounter can shake them out of the tranquility they experienced a while back. If someone is guiding another when such a thing happens, there is bound to be felt a surprising exclamation in their talks.

But imagine if the person guiding you knows exactly what is about to happen in the near future. This exactly is what Mother experiences. She knows my future and there is no rudely cautious response from her. It is very rare.

This is because I am predestined to heaven and most of the things or incidents or elements in my life are. Every time I offer my prayers daily, I am led into the things predestined for me beforehand. Hence, the element of surprise or over cautious feeling is missing in Mother's talks while she is guiding me.

She's just very composed and her voice does not waver.

Typical statements

1. Be brave

Explanations

1. Be brave

I have been prayerless up to the first demonic possession in my life. After being delivered from this, there are other areas where I need deliverance even now. It is ongoing and everybody needs deliverance in their life. This is a fact.

During this ongoing deliverance, there have been many spells of distress I have faced. Demons work through threatening, bringing fear and self-doubt among other things in one's life. I constantly experienced this.

To elaborate on their threatening mode of operation in my life, they bring doubts concerning my anointing or identity in Christ or fear of becoming famous. It is not as if real demons with tails and a beastly figure engages in these activities.

But I experience known people in the family constantly threatening. They do not do it. To be precise, it is not real, but what I perceive.

For example, if I want to bring to the people's notice and proclaim about a recent revelation I received through Mother, they threaten through known family members that what if the masses will not accept that I am a Saint or Mother's son. But it is a routine thing for me and I'm used to it.

And I receive revelations constantly related to elections

or answers to people's prayers or anything.

More so, Mother did not ever ask me to be brave and not worry about the reaction of my brother or sister or mother regarding revealing my identity in Christ publicly or sharing my spiritual journey with everyone. She is a very nice person to be with.

Conclusion

It is quite common with humans to be rude as they get into circumstances and emotions all the time in their everyday dealings with people. But it is very uncommon with Mother. She, as such, does not get shaken out of the blue. This sudden knee-jerk reaction is missing in her talks with me and she is always prepared to come up with a response for anything that comes by to harm.

CHAPTER THIRTEEN

Wise and Exhortative

Mother's stance on everything in God's good wide world is very unique. I have benefited from her wisdom. She can settle any disputes, quarrels, distress and troubles in a very unique way in just minutes. I have never seen anyone as wise as her in the whole world. She is a model for everyone who can call themselves intellectuals as many of her great Saints found her out to be thus.

I can enumerate two incidents in my life:

One is when I was walking around restlessly in my living room thinking about why God works through elaborate plans in my life and not in others, I heard Mother's voice clearly. She startled me with her wisdom that elaborate plans are required in my life and good things can work with time.

To clarify more, she revealed that some time is needed with these plans for her to win favour for me in the eyes of people around to generate a blessing. Imagine, some people admire someone who has a great grit and determination.

Hence to show this grit in me to such a person, she

reveals my character and steely determination in a period of time or through a number of gritty incidents through which I have overcome.

It is clearly understood that a person's mettle is proven through hardships and bad times. So, Mother needs time to work this blessing of me winning favour in the eyes of such people who admire psychological toughness that I have borne.

Gradually, through a number of incidents like these people like this would respect me.

According to her, this is just one kind of blessing that requires time to realize fully.

The second incident is around a time when I started going to the church after a very long gap of three years. This was because hearing holy mass had many restrictions since the period of the pandemic. People were scared to set foot in the church owing to fear of catching the bug of Covid19.

Even family members used to discourage anyone of their dear ones from attending mass in the local church. True to this wisdom, many had perished because of the vagaries of the pandemic attending the church during this period. These victims were both young and old alike.

I got into the habit of hearing online masses to remain safe and this kind of routine continued. But to say the least, there were no large amounts of graces when compared to hearing the mass physically present inside the church. It was just a less viable alternative for the pandemic period.

Later, after many years, I was inspired in the spirit to go to mass, after all the ill-effects and the poignant nature of the pandemic subsided.

So, here I am, taking my sister's motorbike to the church and I did it for a few days. It was feasible to ride the bike to the church as reaching the church on the motorable road takes just 10 minutes. But, commuting by bus and waiting for it and walking the last mile takes 45 minutes.

I was very apprehensive and could not trade going to the church daily with anything else. But my sister and mother were against it because I did not have a driving license. They resisted and after a few days hid the keys of the motorbike.

A great indignant feeling erupted in me. Actually, this was a bondage to create unrest in the family and use me more for the evil powers' resistance to God's kingdom. Being very angry, I started digging all their past and prayerlessness being the cause of problems at home.

This lasted for a few days; a typical unrest loomed large and I did not find peace in my mind too as to why would they put a stumbling block to me going to mass. It was very important to go to mass for me to tackle bondages in my life and family.

Mother made me understand in one minute that they were against me riding the motorbike without license and not mocking my riding skills or simple nature. The moment she revealed this, there was a great calm in my mind.

This is her wisdom and she promised me that she would help me go to the church by bus. Everything settled down as she said and my mind turned peaceful- the demons lost their foothold.

Typical statements

1. I'm your Mother first

Explanations

1. I'm your Mother first

Many times, I ponder over the greatness of God and his omnipotence along with Mother's title of 'Our Lady'. I am much intrigued by the fact that being of such immense character, God and Mother come to my aid, considering me very precious in their sight. It is true that before I had known her to be in images and statues without speaking a word. But this is a reality I live in. She talks to me all the time along with God and both call me their son.

They call me a son as I don't ask for anything in prayer but their will and even though I want something, I make sure it comes through their own hands according to their will. Also, both of them say that I am holy.

Holiness, as anyone should understand, is doing the will of God perfectly and nothing else. Not even the way we dress or follow his commands or behave in a certain way or being anointed to be his people.

Jesus considered to do the will of the Father as his food [John 4:34]. Even many of his Saints like St Faustina perfectly pleased the Father because she considered holiness is to do the same perfectly.

By this standard, I can be called very holy per se. And more so, I am her family and have the title of a Saint.

God is a King and as amply recorded in history, Kings confer titles on the people close to them as 'friend of the king' or more. Here, in this case, God confers titles and honour to certain people close to him viz., Saints, friend like Abraham or more.

Mother deftly brushes aside such thoughts of mine considering her greatness. She clarifies, 'I'm your Mother first'. And this is true. Her attitude is never Queenly or Lady-like but she seeks my love from deep within. Again, a holy attribute.

To corroborate this, she has a pet name for me that is used often by her upon times when finding me cute and pleasing. It translates to 'fat child'. But most commonly, otherwise, she addresses me as 'child' or 'son'. I do love it and she knows that too.

Conclusion

Mother's wisdom is rare and she is very sure of what she says. It is like a never-mistaken logic; no one can deny it. If one hears her talks, they are bound to say that she is heavenly and not human. Only a heavenly bearing can bring such absolute attributes.

Considering her great attributes, even many books are not enough to contain it. But an attempt should be made to make it known. Nothing should be lost into oblivion. She breathes life into books that sound mundane and a chore to read.

CHAPTER FOURTEEN

Acknowledges Sacrifices

Mother herself has made many great sacrifices for the sake of her people. She offered her womb for God's plan of redemption for mankind. Also, she offered the child of her own to be sacrificed for the whole humanity as a blemish less lamb to open the doors of heaven for even the gentiles.

Even her heavenly time is spent for doing good for the human race by serving God eternally as a Queen Mother of Davidic lineage. All of these sacrifices reflect her attitude of serving and being in service of God.

Once I offered some hard sacrifice of my desires for her. It was somewhat dear to me. Mother, just then, showed me a vision of two roses being kept on the family altar. I understood that this sacrifice meant to be dear to her.

She finds value in the sacrifice of each one who is close to her. It pleases her.

Typical statements

1. I can count your wrongs

Explanations

1. I can count your wrongs; they are many

There are many instances wherein I get carried away because of incitement from the demonic influences and somewhat indignantly speak things to people which I ought not to. These may be their laxity as revealed through me through many spiritual mysteries that they are not aware of.

They being unawares, cause me many hindrances in my spiritual life and because of sheer frustration I cannot: digest the same; tolerate it; be patient about it. These whole episodes are overarching to me and bring a great amount of their culpability regarding the same to the fore.

Such mysteries, though they expose the real punishing nature of the spiritual realm and reveal the cause of many situations, illnesses, malicious behaviour of people around, are hidden from sight. The demonic world operates discreetly abetting this.

Though I show these signs of speaking such hurting words, Mother never counts these as wrongs because I suffer for her work. She cherishes all the sufferings I have underwent and is pleased.

Mother never reminds me of these weaknesses and

deficiencies again and again. The fact that I have helped her release over 200 souls from purgatory makes her highly pleased. Though she shows as to being aware of this, I do not mention it.

It is for God and his glory. Love should not boast [1Corinthians 13:4]. More so, everything I have is his and I should not have a say in it about what he should do with my life. She corrects me when I say, 'I'm pleased' that the right words to say are 'I'm happy'. She finds me cute though when I say these words.

Conclusion

Mother has revealed to me many times that she loves my heart and even God does too. This is because I love him very much with my whole heart and my whole life is testimony to it. I take great risks for him and can do anything that entail great difficulty.

Maybe the small wrongs I commit are immaterial to her as she gets the bigger picture of me suffering and doing everything in my strength to glorify God. There does not remain any grim picture of these sufferings too but a whole message of love towards him and for my brethren.

"We love because he first loved us"
1John 4:19

Epilogue

Mother wants all her children to be led to God and give him the glory. She has consecrated herself totally to the service of God since her time on earth. It is not her attitude to seek glory for herself but be a faint reflection of God's glory. There is nothing that she hasn't given for the service of mankind.

Also, she is Our Lady and Davidic Queen Mother, but not equal to God in any sense. As many Saints like Louis Montfort have put forth before, she has been raised to a highest honour a creature can be given.

Her titles are because of her closeness to God. She is the Mother of our Lord; called Blessed by all generations; the Co-Redemptrix and everything that seems good to the Father in service of mankind.

Her main motto is of service and her voice is nothing but the reflection of many characteristics from God. She is wholly and purely the perfect vessel of God he intended to bear him for the period of nine months; consecrated fully for him; not used for any other purpose.

She continues to groom her Saints to be the same too- be fully consecrated and useful for the service of God. Being the Queen of Angels and Saints, these are assisted through the rich graces bestowed on herself while she sojourned the earth.

Mother is full of grace and highly favoured [Luke 1:28]

for the sake of humanity, bringing generations closer to God because of the legacy left behind by her Saints. The Church is richly blessed because of her and them.

And the work is still ongoing with her voice constantly guiding them towards the light i.e., Jesus. Her voice reflects everything from the heavenly kingdom of God giving a glimpse of what is awaiting the wise and faithful servant after his earthly sojourn [Matthew 24:45–47].